Number 1 Teacher

A School Counting Book

Written by Steven L. Layne and Deborah Dover Layne
Illustrated by Doris Ettlinger

For Kristen Stombres and Jerry Johns,
two exceptional educators who trained me well
and always believed in my potential.

DEBBIE

For my treasured friend, Donna Sarich.
When I think of a teacher who is truly #1,
you have always rushed to mind…and you always will.

STEVE

❧

To Karhn White

DORIS

The authors would like to express deep appreciation to the following individuals for their assistance in the initial brainstorming session for this book:

Margaret Boscaljon, Sally Boscaljon, Jodie Bradney, Diana Campos, Rene Chinn, Gail Dover, Michael Graham, Ben Grey, Karen Grey, Patti Hutton, Janet Kmieciak, Lea Anne Roach, Sue Roberts, Kristen Stombres, and Joy Towner

Sleeping Bear Press
310 North Main Street, Suite 300
Chelsea, MI 48118
www.sleepingbearpress.com

© 2008 Sleeping Bear Press is an imprint of Gale, a part of Cengage Learning.

Printed and bound in China.

First Edition

10 9 8 7 6 5 4 3 2 1

Library of Congress Cataloging-in-Publication Data

Layne, Steven L.
Number 1 teacher: a school counting book / written by Steven L. Layne and Deborah Dover Layne; illustrated by Doris Ettlinger.
p. cm.
Summary: "This book uses numbers to introduce readers to material taught in elementary school such as geography (2 north poles), math (telling time), science (3 states of matter), physical education (9 on a baseball team) and others"—Provided by publisher.
Includes bibliographical references.
ISBN 978-1-58536-307-0
1. Counting—Juvenile literature. 2. Mathematics—Study and teaching (Elementary) I. Layne, Deborah Dover. II. Title.

QA113.L38 2008
513.2'11—dc22   2007049890

0—a number we think of as nothing,
but turn that idea around.
It's also the age at which learning begins.
And home's the first "school" where our knowledge is found.

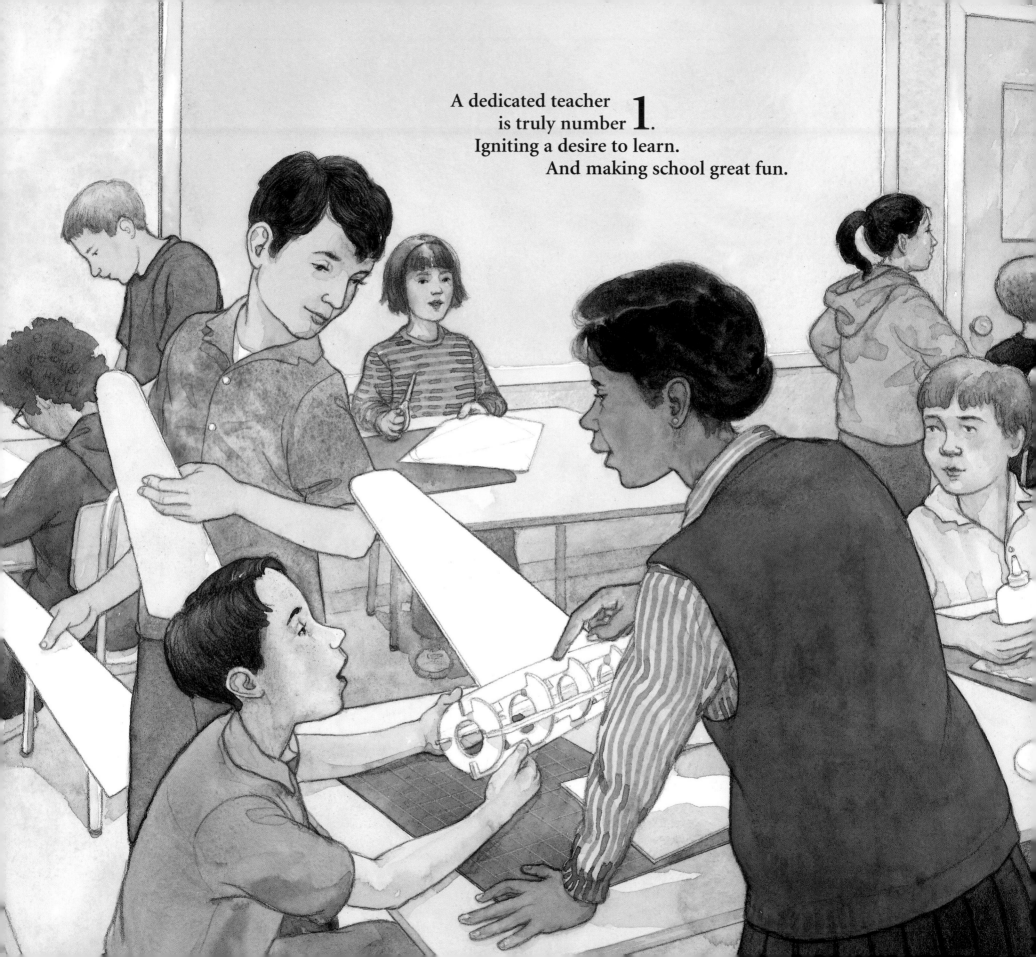

A dedicated teacher
is truly number **1**.
Igniting a desire to learn.
And making school great fun.

Teachers love to help children learn. They are good at explaining things and help prepare their students to live and work in the world. Teachers are an important part of the community.

Teachers are patient, kind, and encouraging. They work hard and always try to make learning fun and interesting.

In the United States, an apple is a traditional gift for a teacher. Did you ever wonder how this practice came to be? It started way back in the sixteenth century. Because teachers were not paid very well, parents would say "thank you" with a gift of food. Apples were usually plentiful and students often gave teachers a basket of apples. As teachers started to earn more, the gift became just one apple to show a student's appreciation.

one
1

2 of the world's most famous locations—
the northern and southern poles
are useful in finding some key destinations—
one of geography's primary goals.

In social studies class, students learn about maps and geography. In science class, students learn what causes day and night. These two subject areas come together when learning about the North and South Poles. On a globe or map of the world, the South Pole is located at the bottom and the North Pole is located at the top.

A huge frozen ocean, the Arctic, surrounds the North Pole and is known as the Arctic region. A vast area of frozen land called Antarctica surrounds the South Pole. These polar lands are among the coldest places on Earth. Many parts are covered in snow and ice all year round.

The axis of the Earth is not upright. Instead, it is tilted. Because it is tilted, the poles have opposite seasons. For example, when it is summer in the Arctic, it is winter in the Antarctic.

two
2

Matter is anything that takes up space, and it comes in three common forms: solids, liquids, and gases. Scientists refer to these forms as the "three states of matter."

Tiny particles called molecules are packed tightly together in solids like books, backpacks, and buildings. This is why solids have shapes. Solids feel hard to the touch because the molecules don't have much space to move around.

Liquids like milk, juice, water, oil, and honey have no shape of their own. Instead, a liquid takes the shape of whatever container holds it. Liquid matter can flow because its molecules have room to move around.

Gas molecules are even farther apart. Gases float around and spread out in all directions. Gases do not have a shape. Some gases are colored and are easily seen, but most gases cannot be seen by the human eye. Two gases you might know about are helium and oxygen. Balloons are sometimes filled with a gas called helium which makes them rise. Oxygen is the most important gas in the atmosphere. Without it plants, animals, and people could not live on planet Earth.

three

3

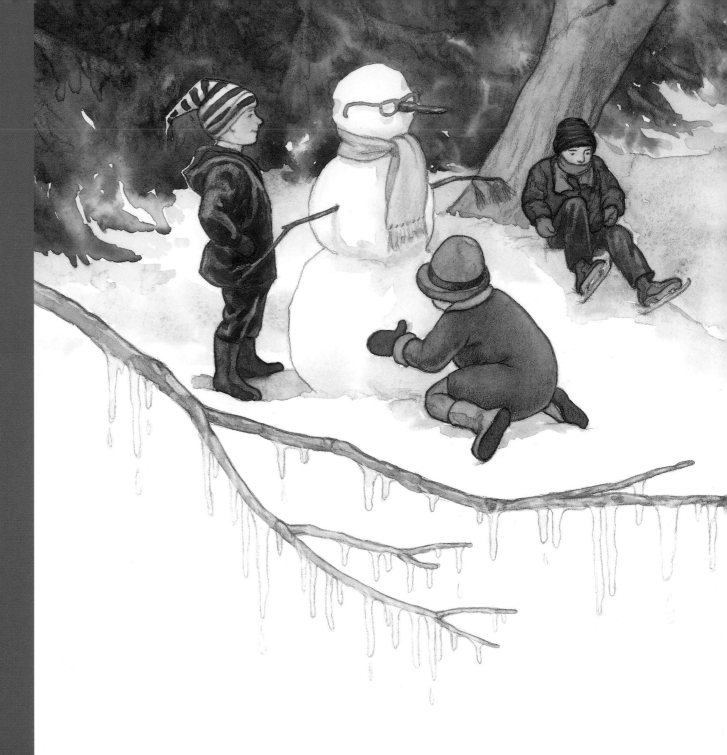

3 common states of matter
can be found in science class—
one is liquid, two is solid
and the third is gas.

Mount Rushmore is one of the largest monuments in the United States. It is carved on a large granite cliff overlooking the Black Hills of western South Dakota.

In the 1920s people in South Dakota were looking for ways to bring visitors to their state. Gutzon Borglum was hired to begin work on a monument. Borglum chose to sculpt the heads of George Washington, Thomas Jefferson, Abraham Lincoln, and Theodore Roosevelt because of the social and political ideals they represented.

George Washington was America's first president and was known for his courage, leadership, and battlefield skill. He was also an important figure in the creation of the U.S. Constitution which represents the spirit of government by the people. Washington is often referred to as "the father of our country."

Thomas Jefferson was president from 1801-1809 and was largely responsible for writing the Declaration of Independence. He also doubled the size of the United States by negotiating the Louisiana Purchase.

four

4

4 is the number of faces
carved in a mountain of stone.
Jefferson, Roosevelt, Lincoln, and Washington
high on Mt. Rushmore are very well known.

Abraham Lincoln is remembered for his beliefs in a united nation and freedom for everyone. He held the nation together during the Civil War and was also largely responsible for ending slavery.

Theodore Roosevelt was president from 1901-1909 and represented the connecting of East and West for his part in the creation of the Panama Canal. He was also a champion of natural resources and created many national parks.

Carving Mount Rushmore was not easy. The workers had to be suspended high in the air as they carved and sculpted the heads using hammers and chisels. They climbed hundreds of steps to get to work each day. The men drilled holes in the granite and then placed dynamite in the holes to blast away huge portions of rock. Altogether it took 14 years and almost one million dollars to finish the monument. It was completed on October 31, 1941.

Mount Rushmore stands 5,725 feet tall. Each face is 60 feet high. Every year workers protect the monument by fixing any cracks that appear. Today, people travel from all over the world to visit Mount Rushmore.

Melodies and harmonies are played, sung, and practiced in music class. Melody is a series of tones arranged in a particular pattern. Often the pattern is so catchy that the melody can be remembered long after the music is over. Harmony is created when two or more different tones are sounded at the same time.

Tones are represented by symbols called notes. The letters A, B, C, D, E, F, and G are used to name the notes. The interval between two notes with the same name is called an octave.

In written music, notes are placed on a staff. A staff is made up of five parallel, horizontal lines and the spaces between them. From bottom to top, the spaces are labeled with the letters F, A, C, and E. The lines (from bottom to top) are labeled with the letters E, G, B, D, and F. Music teachers help students remember the order of these lines by teaching them a catchy phrase like **E**very **G**ood **B**oy **D**eserves **F**udge.

five
5

The **5** lines on a music staff
give notes a place to go.
Without them singers couldn't sing
and trumpets couldn't blow.

G B F C E

In 1984 a group of 17 teachers in the Beaverton, Oregon school district decided to record what has become known as "The Six Traits of Good Writing." The six traits include ideas, organization, voice, word choice, sentence fluency, and conventions. Educators all across America teach their students to use the six traits in their writing.

Ideas are the heart of good writing. They carry the author's message, information, or story line. Organization is the design and structure that holds a piece of writing together. Voice helps the reader feel like he knows the writer because it feels like the writer is speaking to him.

Good word choice makes writing understandable and clear. Words paint a picture for readers or evoke feelings, moods, likes, or dislikes. Sentence fluency describes the rhythm and flow of the language used by the writer and is measured by how easy it is to read the writing out loud. The trait called conventions includes using correct spelling, punctuation, capitalization, and grammar.

six

6

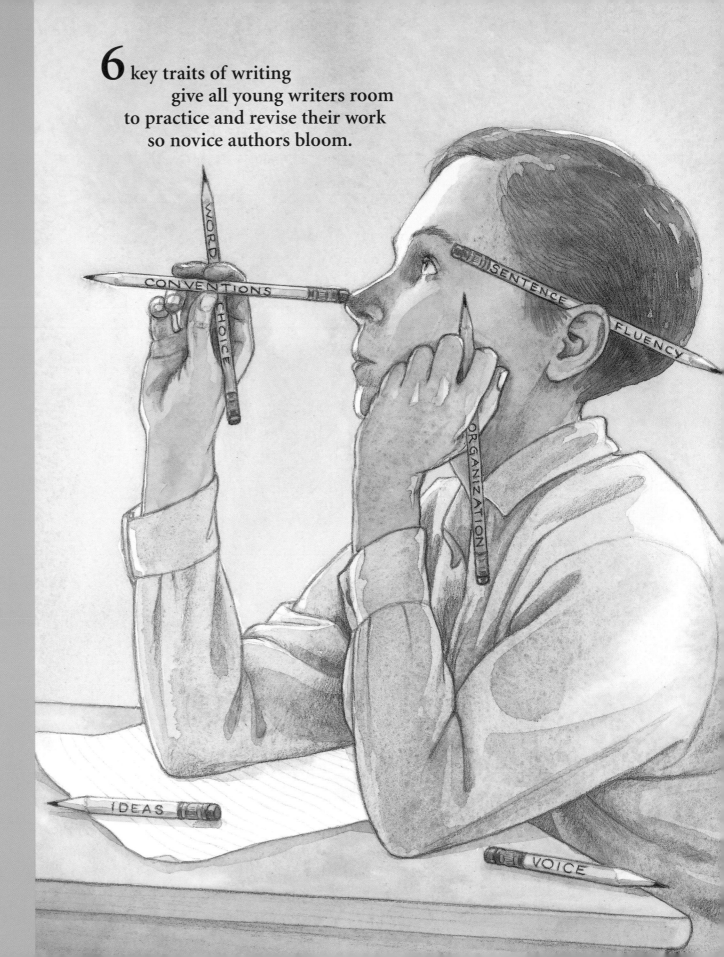

6 key traits of writing
  give all young writers room
to practice and revise their work
  so novice authors bloom.

In school they tell you Roy G. Biv's
a name you need to know.
He stands for 7 colors that
make up every rainbow.

A rainbow is an arc of colors that appears in the sky when raindrops have sunlight cast upon them. To see a rainbow you must have sun to your back and raindrops in front of you. The sun shines through the water droplets and comes out the other side as colors in the sky. Red is always at the top of the rainbow. Orange, yellow, green, blue, indigo, and violet follow—in that order.

Art teachers have an acronym they use to help students remember this color order. Students can think of a character named Roy G. Biv to help them. In the name Roy G. Biv, each letter of the character's name represents the first letter in the color's name.

Mixing light is similar to mixing paint in art class. Mixing red and yellow makes orange. This is why orange lies between red and yellow in a rainbow. Mixing yellow and blue will create green. Each color in a rainbow blends into the next color.

seven
7

Each word in a sentence has a specific job or function. Some words describe, some connect ideas, and some provide action. We call these jobs the parts of speech. The eight main parts of speech are nouns, pronouns, verbs, adjectives, adverbs, prepositions, conjunctions, and interjections.

Nouns name people, places, and things. The words *children*, *park*, and *book* are examples of nouns. Pronouns are substitutes for nouns. They save writers from repeating the same words over and over again. *He*, *she*, and *it* are pronouns.

There are two kinds of verbs. They are called action verbs and linking verbs. Action verbs like *run* or *walk* tell what's happening in a sentence. Linking verbs like *am* or *be* describe a "state of being."

Adjectives describe nouns or pronouns. Adverbs are also describing words. They describe verbs, adjectives, or other adverbs.

Prepositions connect nouns and pronouns to the rest of the sentence. Conjunctions are different kinds of connectors that link individual words, sentences, clauses, or words within a clause. Interjections are used to put strong feeling into a sentence.

eight

8

The sentences that we create use parts of speech that number **8**.

9 Nine innings in a baseball game,
players fielding balls.
Plus fans who holler loudly
and evaluate the umpire's calls.

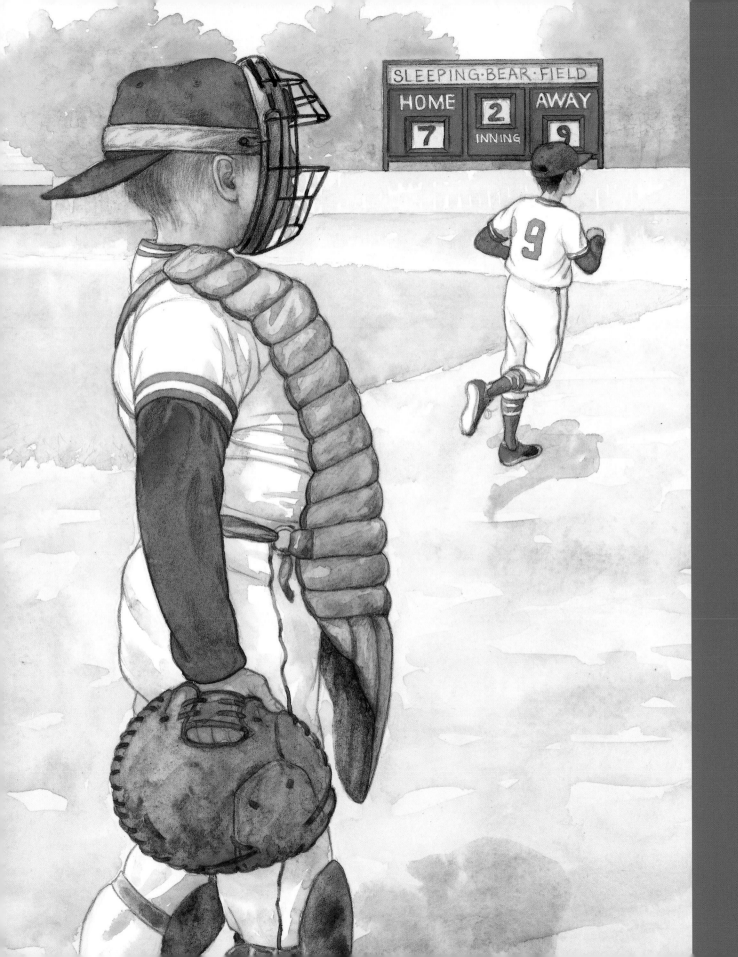

SLEEPING·BEAR·FIELD

HOME 7 | 2 INNING | AWAY 9

Physical education is often a favorite part of the day for many students because they get a chance to be active and loud. It is also called "gym" class or P.E.

The gym teacher demonstrates basic skills for playing games like baseball and many other activities. Gym class might include jogging, swimming, gymnastics, strength training, and dancing.

Gym teachers are proud of their students' accomplishments and help them learn to be graceful winners and losers. Students who show good sportsmanship play fairly and treat their opponents with respect and courtesy.

Helping students learn how to stay physically fit is another important part of the gym teacher's job. This is accomplished by teaching students about good eating habits and proper exercise. These are important virtues to learn in order to be healthy for life.

nine
9

In math class students learn about measurement. In different times and parts of the world, there have been many systems of measurement. Today, only two systems are commonly used. In the United States the *customary* or *inch-pound system* is used, but the *metric system* is used almost everywhere else in the world.

In the United States length is measured in inches, feet, yards, and miles. In the metric system, length is measured in millimeters, centimeters, meters, and kilometers. Soccer fields throughout the world are a standard 100 meters long. Athletes run the 100-yard dash during a track meet. Signs on the roadways give distances in miles or kilometers depending on what country the signs are posted.

The original metric system was adopted by France in 1795. The current metric system is also called the "International System of Units" or *SI* for short. The metric system is based on the number 10. For example, there are 10 decimeters in a meter, 10 centimeters in a decimeter, and 10 millimeters in a centimeter.

ten

10

Measuring in metric
means the number **10** will rule.
Though not our country's system
it's still introduced in school.

The **11**th of November—
an important holiday
is set aside to honor those
who've fought to keep us safe today.

On November 11th people celebrate Veterans Day in the United States. This holiday honors men and women who have served in the United States military. The military is made up of the Army, Navy, Air Force, Coast Guard, and the Marine Corps. Brave people who have worked to protect our country through their service in the military are called veterans.

Veterans Day is a time for people to remember the sacrifices veterans have made and to thank them for risking their lives to protect the United States. We also remember and honor those who have died while trying to gain or protect our freedom.

President Dwight Eisenhower and Congress declared November 11th to be Veterans Day in 1954. Many people watch parades, listen to speeches and fly American flags on Veterans Day. Some people visit monuments and graves and take a moment of silence to honor those who have died. Special services are held at the Tomb of the Unknown Soldier in Arlington National Cemetery in Arlington, Virginia.

eleven
11

In the United States, schools are classified as elementary or secondary. Most elementary schools contain grades kindergarten through fifth or sixth grade. In elementary school, students build a foundation for future learning.

When students leave elementary school, they usually move on to a middle school or junior high that contains some combination of grades 5-8. Junior high schools introduce students to the kind of class schedule and assignments they will find in high school.

Most high schools (9th-12th grade) offer classes to students who are planning to go to college and to those wanting immediate training in specific job skills. College preparatory programs consist of subjects like math, history, language, and the physical and social sciences. The four years of high school are referred to as freshman, sophomore, junior, and senior years. At the end of 12th grade, students participate in a formal graduation ceremony.

twelve
12

Grade **12**'s the final year in school.
You'll likely hear that "Seniors rule!"
The lessons started in grade K
complete on Graduation Day.

A **20** we count on for getting things done
are the twenty-four hours that make a day run.
Though you only see twelve when you look at the clock,
the hands go 'round *twice* as they tick and they tock.

In elementary math class students learn how to tell time. Time is a measure of the hours, days, months, and years. We measure time so that we can keep track of the things that happen in our lives. For example, we need to know what time school begins and ends as well as what time the bus will arrive at the bus stop.

Clocks measure time. A clock has two hands. The long hand tells the minutes, and the short hand marks the hours. A day contains 24 hours, but a clock's face only shows 12. The hour hand circles the clock twice in a day because each day has two parts. These parts are called A.M. and P.M. The abbreviation A.M. represents the period of time from midnight until 12 noon. The letters P.M. represent the period of time from noon until midnight.

The shortest unit of time we measure is called a second. There are 60 seconds in each minute and 60 minutes in an hour. A stop watch measures minutes and seconds. They are often used to measure time in athletic races or events.

twenty
20

Temperature is a measure of how hot or cold something is. Hot things have a high temperature, and cold things have a low temperature. In science class, students measure temperature with a tool called a thermometer.

There are different kinds of thermometers. Some have small windows that indicate the temperature with digital numbers. Parents and nurses may use this type of thermometer in a child's ear to measure body temperature. Some thermometers are filled with red-dyed alcohol. The red liquid in a thermometer rises as temperatures get warmer.

Temperature is measured in *degrees*. There are two different systems for measuring temperature. The mercury thermometer used today was invented in 1714 by German scientist Gabriel Fahrenheit. The scale of degrees is named after him. On this scale, water freezes at 32 degrees. Water boils at 212 degrees. In the United States, temperature is measured in degrees Fahrenheit.

The rest of the world uses a different system called the Celsius scale. It was named after Swedish professor Anders Celsius who invented the Celsius thermometer. On the Celsius scale water freezes at 0 degrees, and it boils at 100 degrees.

For **30** we'll travel to science class
and at thirty-two degrees
    the Fahrenheit scale will give us a chill;
        it's the temperature at which water will freeze.

In social studies class, elementary students study a topic known as *westward expansion*. Westward expansion tells the story of how our country grew larger over time. The original 13 colonies were located on the east coast of the United States—right on the Atlantic Ocean. As our country grew, it gained new land that was always located to the west of the original 13 colonies.

In the 1840s California was part of Mexico. The United States government wanted access to Pacific Ocean seaports. Following a war between the U. S. and Mexico over the western land, the two countries signed a peace treaty. This treaty gave parts of present day California, Texas, New Mexico, Nevada, Utah, and Arizona to the United States. In return the U.S. paid about 15 million dollars for this land. The signers of the treaty did not know that gold had been discovered in California just a few days earlier.

forty
40

40 gives us forty-niners—
Gold Rush Fever struck these miners.
Heading west to carve their niche
sure that they would strike it rich.

Also in the 1840s a pioneer trader named John Sutter received a land grant of 50,000 acres located on the American River in the Sacramento Valley. He built on this land, and it became known as Sutter's Fort. Sutter hired a carpenter named James Marshall to build a sawmill about 45 miles northeast, and the new sawmill became known as Sutter's Mill. In 1948 Marshall discovered the first gold nuggets at Sutter's Mill.

Word of this discovery spread quickly. People rushed to the hills and rivers of California from all over the world to find gold in hopes of becoming wealthy. Gold seekers caused California's population to increase from about 15,000 to nearly 100,000 by the end of 1849. This population explosion in 1849 is why gold seekers came to be known as the *forty-niners*!

The California gold rush was one of the most important events in American history. It caused many changes in American lives. It completed westward expansion to the Pacific Ocean, gave identity to the new state of California, and opened new routes of transportation.

The **50** stars on our nation's flag
represent each state.
The allegiance we pledge for unity
has helped to make our country great.

The American flag can be found in most classrooms. The flag is a symbol of freedom. It stands for the land, people, and government of the United States.

On June 14, 1777, the Continental Congress passed the first law about the flag. The flag had thirteen red and white stripes and thirteen white stars on a blue background. Red represents courage, and white stands for purity and goodness. Blue stands for justice. As the United States grew, more stars were added to the flag. Today there are 50 stars on the flag—one for each state. The thirteen stripes still represent the original 13 colonies.

In many American classrooms children recite the Pledge of Allegiance. It is a promise of loyalty to our country. Reciting the pledge got its start in 1888 when a magazine called *The Youth's Companion* asked children to assist with a special project to help buy flags for their schools. Their idea was to celebrate the 400th anniversary of Columbus's arrival in America in 1892 which would be called Columbus Day. Children would raise their flags and together recite the Pledge of Allegiance which Francis Bellamy had written for this special occasion.

fifty
50

In art class, students use crayons to create bright, colorful drawings. A crayon is a stick of colored wax that is shaped like a short pencil. Usually, crayons come in boxes of 8, 16, 24, 48, or 64. Crayons are often the first drawing tool children learn to use.

Crayons are made in a factory. They begin as clear wax. In the factory, the wax is heated in large tanks until it melts into liquid form. Then, pipes carry the liquid wax into big pots called vats, and a worker adds colored powder called pigment. Many vats are used, each containing a different color. Next, the colored wax is poured into crayon-shaped molds where it stays until it cools and hardens. Then a worker takes the crayons out of the mold and checks each one for chips and dents. Any crayons that are damaged are melted and molded again. The perfect crayons will be sent to machines that wrap paper labels around them, sort the colors, and then box them for shipment to many different stores.

60 shows us a popular treat—
with sixty-four colors the set is complete
For bringing a picture or project to life
there's nothing like crayons to do the job right.

sixty
60

In many elementary schools, students may choose to play a musical instrument and join a band or orchestra. There are three main groups of instruments in a school band. These include the woodwinds, the brass, and the percussion instruments. Each of these groups is called a family because all of the instruments are related to each other in important ways. A school orchestra is made of up these three families plus the string family of instruments.

The string family is the largest in the orchestra. The most common members of the string family from smallest to largest are the violin, the viola, the cello, and the bass.

Most woodwind instruments have a mouthpiece that contains a reed, and they look like narrow tubes with a row of holes in them. Some popular woodwind instruments include the clarinet, flute, saxophone, and oboe.

The instruments in the brass family are all made of a shiny metal called brass. Some popular brass instruments include the trumpet, the trombone, the French horn, and the tuba.

Percussion instruments are played by striking or shaking them. Some percussion instruments like the snare or bass drum are used for keeping rhythm.

A musical instrument makes a fine **70**—
seventy-six trombones to be exact.
And while they *led* the parade on "old Broadway"
in the school band they're found in the back.

A music teacher instructs children about different types of music, singing and listening skills, and musical instruments. It's the music teacher's job to help students learn the basic elements of music including melody, harmony, tempo, and rhythm. Melody is the way musical sounds or tones are arranged to create a catchy tune. Harmony is the way two or more sounds go together. Tempo is the speed at which music is played, and rhythm is the pattern of long and short sounds.

Music teachers use instruments like the xylophone, drums, triangle, tambourine, and recorder to teach their students. The most common instrument used by a music teacher is the piano.

The piano is a popular keyboard instrument that has 88 keys. The black and white keys are arranged in a pattern. The keys on the left side of the keyboard play notes with a lower pitch. The keys on the right play higher notes. Inside the piano are strings and tiny felt-covered hammers. Sound is made when the keys are pressed down causing the hammers to strike the strings.

eighty
80

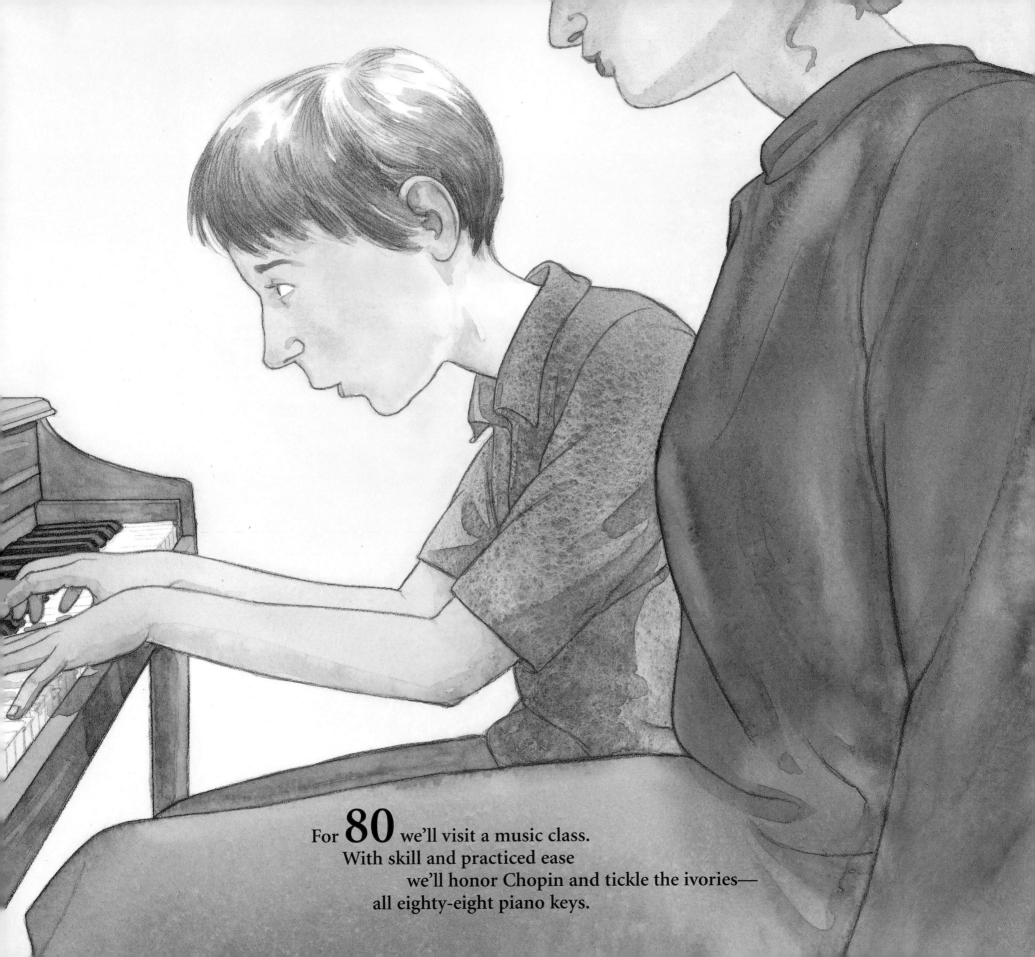

For **80** we'll visit a music class.
With skill and practiced ease
    we'll honor Chopin and tickle the ivories—
all eighty-eight piano keys.

Geometry is a type of math that involves studying the shape, size, and position of lines, angles, curves, and figures. Geometric shapes can be found in the environment in both nature and in objects made by people. Some examples of geometric shapes include circles, cones, squares, rectangles, cubes, triangles, and spheres.

Shapes can be found everywhere. Wheels, coins, and a full moon are examples of circular shapes. Rectangles and squares have four corners and four straight edges. Playing cards, envelopes, checker boards and cereal boxes are examples of these shapes. Triangles are shapes that have three sides and three corners. A slice of pie, cheese, or pizza, and the sails on a boat can be shaped like a triangle.

An angle is a wedge-shaped piece formed between two crossing lines. In math class students measure angles with a tool called a protractor which is marked off in a measure called degrees. Angles that make square corners and measure 90 degrees are called *right angles*.

ninety
90

Geometry's tough from a certain angle
    but what's kind of easy is a right triangle.
90 degrees—a right angle's measure
    gives the math students a great deal of pleasure.

In the primary grades students learn to count. Many teachers have a counting chart displayed in the classroom. Teachers often begin the day by having students add a link or tally mark to the chart. The goal is for students to count the days of school until they reach 100.

Students look forward to the 100th day of school because their teachers usually plan a big celebration for this special day. During the celebration students usually enjoy a special treat, a story reading, and other meaningful activities. To contribute to the festivities, students are frequently asked to bring a collection of 100 items to school. Some good examples of collections to share with classmates might include 100 paperclips, 100 rubber bands, 100 pennies, 100 buttons, or 100 marbles. Collection possibilities are only limited by each student's imagination.

Several picture books on this topic have been written for children. Find out more about 100th day of school celebrations by reading *100th Day Worries* by Margery Cuyler, *Fluffy's 100th Day of School* by Kate McMullan, or *Jake's 100th Day of School* by Lester Laminack.

one hundred 100

100 days of school!
A cause for celebration.
Excitement mounts as students count
then shout in jubilation.

There's one more kind of counting
that we just have to do.
Just think—you count on teachers
and teachers count on you!

When we all do our very best,
when we can't be outdone,
that's when the students and the teachers
both are #1.

Bibliography

Adler, D. A. (1999). How tall, how short, how far away. New York: Holiday House.

Ansary, M. T. (1999). Holiday histories: Veterans Day. Des Plaines, IL: Reed Educational & Professional Publishing.

Armbruster, A. (1991). The American Flag. New York: Franklin Watts.

Armentrout, P. (1996). Lights in the sky. Vero Beach, FL: The Rourke Press, Inc.

Ashley, S. (2004). Mount Rushmore. Milwaukee: Weekly Reader Early Learning Library.

Aust, S. (1984). Clocks: How time flies. Minneapolis: Lerner Publications Company.

Bodden, V. (2007). Mount Rushmore. Mankato, MN: Creative Education.

Bonner, N. (1995). Habitats: Polar regions. New York: Thomson Learning.

Bryant, J. (1991). Carol Thomas-Weaver: Music teacher. Frederick, MD: Twenty-First Century Books.

Cuyler, M. (2000). One hundredth day worries. New York: Simon & Schuster.

Forman, M. H. (1997). From wax to crayon. New York: Children's Press.

Fowler, A. (1998). All the colors of the rainbow. New York: Children's Press.

Fowler, A. (1997). The top and bottom of the world. New York: Children's Press.

Fradin, D. B. (1988). The flag of the United States. Chicago: Children's Press.

Gabriel, L. S. (2001). Mount Rushmore: From mountain to monument. Mankato, MN: The Child's World, Inc.

Hunter, R. (2001). Discovering science: Hot and cold. New York: Steck-Vaughn Company.

Hunter, R. (2001). Discovering science: Matter. Austin, TX: Steck-Vaughn Company.

Laminack, L. (2006). Jake's 100th day of school. Atlanta: Peachtree.

Layne, S. L., and D. S. Layne. (2005). T is for teachers. Chelsea, MI: Sleeping Bear Press.

Lehn, B. (2000). What is a teacher? Brookfield, CT: The Millbrook Press.

Lowenstein, F. (2006). What does a teacher do? Berkeley Heights, NJ: Enslow Publishers, Inc.

Lynch, W. (2002). Musical instruments: Keyboards. Chicago: Reed Educational & Professional Publishing.

McKerns, D., and L. Motchkavitz. (1998). The kid's guide to good grammar. Lincolnwood, IL: Lowell House.

McMullan, K. (1999). Fluffy's 100th day of school. New York: Scholastic, Inc.

Monroe, J. (2002). The California gold rush. Mankato, MN: Capstone Press.

Nelson, R. (2003). From wax to crayon. Minneapolis: Lerner Publications Company.

Older, J. (2000). Telling time. Watertown, MA: Charlesbridge Publishing.

Patten, J. M. (1995). Let's wonder about science: Solids, liquids and gases. Vero Beach, FL: The Rourke Book Co., Inc.

Patilla, P. (2000). Math links: Shapes. Des Plaines, IL: Reed Educational & Professional Publishing.

Pillar, M. (1992). Join the band. New York: HarperCollins Publishers.

Quiri, P. R. (1998). The American flag. New York: Children's Press.

Radlauer, R. S. (1992). Honor the flag. Lake Forest, IL: Forest House Publishing Company, Inc.

Ramsay, H. (1998). Hot and cold. New York: Children's Press.

Roy, J. R. (2004). You can write: Using good grammar. Berkeley Heights, NJ: Enslow Publishers, Inc.

Rubin, M., and A. Daniel. (1992). The orchestra. Buffalo, NY: Firefly Books.

Sargent, B. (2007). Hot numbers - cool math. New York: Children's Press.

Schomp, V. (2000). If you were a teacher. New York: Benchmark Books.

Schuh, M. C. (2003). Veterans Day. Mankato, MN: Capstone Press.

Schwartz, D. (2003). Millions to measure. New York: HarperCollins Publishers.

Spandel, V. (2004). Creating young writers: Using the six traits to enrich writing process in primary classrooms. New York: Pearson Education, Inc.

Stille, D. (2004). Matter: See it, touch it, smell it. Minneapolis: Picture Window Books.

Swanson, J. (1990). I pledge allegiance. Minneapolis: Carolrhoda Books.

Taylor, B. (1995). Arctic and Antarctic. New York: Dorling Kindersley Publishing, Inc.

Teitelbaum, M. (2004). Sportsmanship. Chicago: Raintree.

The new book of knowledge. (2007). Danbury, CT: Scholastic Library Publishing, Inc.

Thomas, R. (2002). Keyboards. Chicago: Heinemann Library.

Thompson, L. (2005). Expansion of America: The California gold rush. Vero Beach, FL: Rourke Publishing LLC.

Turner, B. J. (2003). Out and about at the orchestra. Minneapolis: Picture Window Books.

Uschan, M. V. (2003). The California gold rush. Milwaukee: World Almanac Library.

VanSteenwyk, E. (1991). The California gold rush. New York: Franklin Watts.

Vernolia, J. (2000). Kids write right: What you need to know to be a writing powerhouse. Berkeley, CA: Tricycle Press.

Walker, S. M. (2006). Matter. Minneapolis: Lerner Publications Company.

Watts, C. (2002). Polar regions. Charlotte, NC: Stampley Enterprises.

Woods, S. G. (1999). Crayons: From start to finish. Woodbridge, CT: Blackbirch Press, Inc.

Wyler, R. (1989). An outdoor science book: Raindrops and rainbows. Englewood Cliffs, NJ: Simon & Schuster, Inc.

Yates, I. (1997). All about shape. New York: Benchmark Books.